Summary

How To Be An Antiracist

BY

Ibram X. Kendi

D1416141

Table of Contents

Executive Summary

This book by Ibram X. Kendi helps with exactly what the title says i.e. *How to be an antiracist.* Kendi is an author, professor and historian of race and discriminatory policy in America. He is one of the country's leading antiracist voices and is a National Book Award-winning and #1 New York Times bestselling author. He was born to parents who are devout Christians and were inspired greatly by the Black liberation theology themselves. Influenced by the same theories, Kendi's career transitioned from sports journalism to racial justice work after graduating from the Florida A&M University.

In *How to Be An Antiracist*, Kendi meticulously explains what it means to be an antiracist and how declaring yourself 'not-racist' isn't enough at all. Giving historical context wherever possible, the author helps us understand that racism isn't a newborn problem and that its roots are buried deep in the pages of history. He also discusses in detail his own transformations along the journey to becoming an antiracist and explains how the events happening in his daily life opened his eyes to the problems of racism around him. The book covers several aspects of racism from biology and ethnicity to body, behavior and color. Kendi doesn't refrain from pointing his antiracist fingers towards Black racists as much as Whites and clarifies that racism isn't bound to a specific race, class or ethnicity.

This book hopes to bring a newfound awareness to readers regarding the different kinds of racism all around and wishes to inspire them to truly recognize the problem of racism and how to deal with it. It calls for some major mindset shifts when it comes to thinking about races and racism and strives to instill the hope that we can all, one day eventually be antiracists. And finally, it hopes to explain that antiracism is the true solution to the problems of humanity and to forming a better world than what we're used to living in right now.

My Racist Introduction

Attempting to recall my speech at the Prince William County Martin Luther King Jr. oratorical contest is still a nightmare for me. Making it to the final round of this delightful event was a shocker to my parents who never expected much from me. And why would they? I carried a GPA that was lower than 3 and a SAT score that barely surpassed 1000. Besides I had no hope of getting into any renowned college and was, at that moment, riding the wave after being surprisingly admitted to the two colleges I had unenthusiastically applied to.

But my defiant nature and lackluster academic career were much less of a problem than my lack of knowledge about subjects like Shakespeare or the historical significance of the Confederate memorials surrounding me in Manassas, Virginia. Consequently, I couldn't understand why a large number of tourists trekked to Manassas National Battlefield Park to relive the glory of the Confederate victories at the Battles of Bull Run during the Civil War. I was simply ignorant to all this important stuff. But then I never really read much of anything in my high school years.

Delivering that speech itself was a life-changing event for me. I had won my high school competition months before. My confidence levels were also running exceptionally high after acing another country wide competition just weeks earlier. But even with all that confidence, I still wonder if it was my poor sense of self that first generated my poor sense of my people. Or was it a poor sense of my people that inflamed a poor sense of myself? It's like that question about the chicken and the egg which has no right or wrong answer. Nonetheless, the answer is less important than the cycle it describes. In the case of racism, it's usually the racist ideas that make people of color think less of themselves, ultimately making them more vulnerable to racist ideas.

My lack of confidence and subpar academic performance as a student was rooted in the fact that I was made to believe that it was all due to my race. This lack of encouragement further reinforced the notion that Black people, my people, were naturally less studious and strengthened the racist ideas inside me. It took me to the point where I was ready to preach these notions to my own people without questioning the ideas of society that judged us in the first place.

Recalling the racist statements I made in that speech makes me feel ashamed of myself. I can cite myself saying, "Our youth's minds are still in captivity!", when I now believe those minds are in captivity of *racist ideas*. I remember myself proclaiming, "They think it's okay to be those who are most feared in our society!" presuming that it was *their* fault that they were feared. I kept throwing out unproven racist ideas about other things that were wrong with black youth throughout the speech, pumped by the applause of the crowd and the black judge who kept patting me on the back for more.

And I kept giving more.

I failed to realize at the moment that to say something is inferior about a racial group is to say a racist idea. I wasn't serving my people, I was serving racist ideas. I had internalized racism and the racist culture. I was made to think that Black people themselves were the problem instead of the policies that trapped them. This is the same sort of manipulation that can be seen in the racist comments made by President Donald Trump. His use of language manipulates and emphasizes the concept that Black people are a problem in themselves, diverting some much-needed attention from critical policy issues that govern people of color. Even worse, when called out for his racist inclinations, the President confidently denounces his words with a now-predictable pattern.

And that is the heartbeat of racism- *Denial.*

Don't be fooled though. Denial resides within all of us. We reflexively defend having said or done something racist when called out for it ourselves. Many of us who detest the Trumps of the world wouldn't dare accept our own racist ideas. We suffice with being 'not racist', when in reality, that neutral position defies the struggle against racism. A more realistic stance for not being racist is therefore being an 'Antiracist'. The difference lies in the fact that being 'not racist' is racism wearing a mask whereas being an antiracist locates the root problems in power and policies and confronts racial inequalities.

One of the core principles of antiracism is to identify and describe the term 'Racism' consistently in an attempt to dismantle it. This is because merely calling it a 'Pejorative' term which should be avoided only freezes a person into inaction. Just like declaring yourself 'Not racist' implies being a masked racist, failing to see and describe 'Racism' as a term turns one blind to racial inequalities and injustice.

In this book, I share my journey from anti-Black racism to anti-White racism to finally being an antiracist. We already know how to be a racist and how to pretend to be not racist. Now let's learn how to be an antiracist so that humanity can move towards a potential future world with all of its imperfect beauty and glory.

Chapter 1 - Definitions

Key Knowledge Pointers

- For both me and my parents, definitions were a key in transforming our perspectives

- Definitions are immensely important because it is critical to do the basic work of defining the kind of people we want to be in a language that is stable and consistent so we can work toward stable, consistent goals

- It is only once we have a strong understanding of the definitions of racism and antiracism that we can attempt to make sense of racism in the world around us.

My Ma and Dad rediscovered the definition of a 'Christian' through separate revolutionary journeys of their own. This new interpretation of a word that they'd already chosen as their core identity naturally transformed them and shaped their lives to become the Christians that Jesus the Revolutionary inspired them to be.

In 1970, both of my parents were attending the InterVarsity's Urbana '70 at the University of Illinois, albeit unaware of each other's presence. The Black students of the University had succeeded in pushing the InterVarsity Christian Fellowship to dedicate the second night of the conference to Black theology. Black students across the country had arrived to attend the event where Soul Liberation was also scheduled to perform.

My mother and father, Carol and Larry, weren't complete strangers though. They had previously exchanged small talk at a recruiting event for Urbana '70. The event was co-organized by Larry at his Church in Jamaica, Queens. Although attending Urbana '70 was a decision that they took independently of each other, both of them wanted to hear Tom Skinner preach at the event as well as attend the live performance by Soul Liberation.

But each of them had their own reasons for finding Tom Skinner.

Carol came to know about Skinner through his younger brother who was enrolled with her at the Nyack College whereas Larry discovered him through his own pursuit of the Black ideology. After a pulsating performance by Soul Liberation and a powerful speech by Tom Skinner, the event concluded with Skinner's call for evangelical liberators. Both my parents were extremely responsive to this call and attended a series of events that continued over the week of the conference. Each of the meetings that ensued reinforced Skinner's call and Ma and Dad found themselves joining the churchless church of the Black Power movement. Black power had captured my parents in 1970 and they had started thinking about liberating Black people instead of saving them.

Consequently, Ma returned to the Nyack College in the spring of 1971 and helped form a Black student union. She also started embracing her culture more openly and began wearing African clothes. Upon returning to his Church, my Dad also started organizing programs that asked thought provoking questions and began reading the work of James Cone, the scholarly father of Black liberation theology. After making a daring attempt to attend one of Cone's classes at Union Theological Seminary, he asked him a question that changed the course of his entire life forever.

He asked Cone, "*What is your definition of a Christian?*", to which he replied, "*A Christian is one who is striving for liberation.*"

During that spring in 1971, both Ma and Dad had realized that Christianity was about struggle and liberation. And this idea was nothing but revolutionary for themselves and their unborn children.

My own journey towards antiracism started at Urbana '70. My struggle to be an antiracist isn't much different from my parent's religious strivings to be a Christian who battles for liberation. What unites our struggles, and is a key factor in changing our perspectives, is the use of 'Definitions'. Definitions are immensely important because it is critical to do the basic work of defining the kind of people we want to be in a language that is stable and consistent so we can work toward stable, consistent goals.

With that in mind, let's begin with some definitions.

Racism: Racism is a marriage of racist policies and racist ideas that produces and normalizes racial inequities.

Racial inequity: Racial inequity is when two or more racial groups are not standing on approximately equal footing.

Antiracist policy: An antiracist policy is any measure that produces or sustains racial equity between racial groups.

Policy: written and unwritten laws, rules, procedures, processes, regulations, and guidelines that govern people.

Racist policy: A racist policy is any measure that produces or sustains racial inequity between racial groups.

Other terms used for racist policy are 'institutional racism,' 'structural racism,' and 'systemic racism'. These are relatively vague terms. Racism *itself* is institutional, structural, and systemic. Another common phrase being used in this context is "racial discrimination". This also doesn't really address racism to its core because it diverts attention from *racist policies and policymakers*, which are paramount to the problem of racism. Besides, the 'discrimination' part of racial discrimination fails to explain whether that discrimination resulted in equity or inequity. The consequences are clear; if discrimination brought about equity then it's antiracist but if it did the opposite then it's racist. This is why the only remedy to racist discrimination is antiracist discrimination, which implies that in order to treat some folks equally, we must first treat them differently. It's all about recognizing race before eliminating racial inequalities.

Understanding the differences between racist policies and antiracist policies, as well as those between racist ideas and antiracist ideas, allows us to return to our fundamental definitions. And it is only once we have a strong understanding of the definitions of racism and antiracism that we can attempt to make sense of racism in the world around us. For instance, our incompetent climate policies are racist policies because more people of color are affected by the climate changes in their regions than White people. Another prevalent example of racial inequality is that Black lives, that live an average of 3.5 years less than an average White life and are more prone to certain health conditions, consistently lie at the receiving end of poor health policies and insurance.

It is now up to us to decide which side of the history we want to be on. Racism and antiracism are akin to peelable name tags that can be put on or removed on purpose. No one becomes a racist or antiracist. We can only strive to become either one, knowingly or unknowingly. But being an antiracist not only requires persistent self-awareness, constant self-criticism, and regular self-examination, but also demands a dramatical reorientation of our consciousness.

Chapter 2 - Dueling Consciousness

Key Knowledge Pointers

- The dueling consciousness in a Black mind fights being two things; antiracist and assimilationist

- The dueling consciousness in a White man fights being two things; segregationist and assimilationist

- Both Black and White dueling consciousness have resulted into their own types of policies

Americans have long been trained to see the shortcomings of people instead of the policies that govern them. This is a very convenient mistake to make because it's easier to see people that are in front of you than the distant policies that shape the lives of these people. My Ma and Dad made the very same mistake.

My parents hadn't seen each other after the bus ride to Urbana '70 but later met at a Soul Liberation concert in 1973. They had sensed the growing intimacy between them and got married eight years later. In 1982, when my mother was expecting her second child i.e. me, President Reagan declared a war on us. He proclaimed that "We must put drug abuse on the run through stronger law enforcement", however, it wasn't exactly drug abuse that got on the run. It was people like me, the Black folks, that were targeted by a regime of *stronger law enforcement*. It wasn't just Reagan that started a war that was directed at people of color. Before him, President Lyndon B. Johnson did the same when he declared 1965 *the year when this country began a thorough, intelligent, and effective war on crime*. Even President Nixon announced his war on drugs in 1971 to wreck his biggest critics i.e. the Blacks and anti war activists.

In the aftermath of Reagan's declaration, the number of Americans in prisons quadrupled between 1980 and 2000. More Americans were jailed for drug crimes than violent crimes every year from 1993 to 2009. Quite unsurprisingly, the percentage of Black people jailed for drug offenses was higher than White people although white people are more likely to sell drugs than Black and Latinx people. The jail time for Black nonviolent drug offenders was typically the same as that of violent White criminals while Black and Latinx people remained grossly overrepresented in the prison population back in 2016.

But the worst part was that Black people and leaders joined with these forces to berate their own folks, convinced that these drug abusers were cancelling out any good that the Civil Rights Movement had done. These Black leaders failed to recognize that their requests for receiving more police officers, tougher and mandatory sentencing, and more jails were being met without an ounce of attention paid to their calls for ending police brutality, more jobs, better schools, and drug-treatment programs.

My parents got entrapped by the same ideas. As Black people who had risen from poverty into the middle class through education and hard work, they were led to believe that these Black criminals took pleasure in stealing and were criminally dependent on their hard-earned money. Like other Black people who had improved their social and financial stature, my parents were told that they must save these 'Ghetto' folks by enlightening them with the importance of hard work, education and respect for family. No one presented any evidence that these ghetto folks lacked such attributes in the first place.

Consequently, my parents focused more on correcting Black people and their behaviors instead of challenging Reagan's policies, and taught me the same. Reagan's policies pushed more Black people into poverty, raised unemployment within Black youth and exposed more Black people to police brutality.

Deep down, my parents still believed in the power of the liberation theology that they had come across in Urbana. However, their reasonable fears prevented them from acting on their dreams of liberation for the Black people so they settled down as American middle class. They wanted to fit in with the White people while maintaining their own identity as Black folks. This state of mind was termed as 'double consciousness' by W.E.B. Du Bois but may be more precisely called 'dueling consciousness'. Desiring to be a Negro while also striving to blend in with White Americans was a grueling struggle happening in one Black body, and it overtook my parents.

This dueling consciousness in a Black mind usually fights between two things; antiracism and assimilationism. While antiracism involves looking at yourself through your own eyes, assimilationism encompasses looking at yourself from the eyes of others i.e. White people in this case. Assimilationist ideas are racist ideas because they typically place White people as the benchmark that Black people should measure themselves against.

This dueling consciousness played itself out in my parents in the form of Black self-reliance. Black self-reliance was a double-edged sword; it was both antiracist and assimilationist. It fed Black pride by emphasizing that there was nothing wrong with Black people and their culture but also instilled shame by insisting that something in the Black behavior needed correction.

White people also have their own dueling consciousness that is divided between being segregationist and assimilationist. A segregationist believes that people of color are incapable of developing and reaching the superior standard that White people can achieve. An assimilationist, on the other hand, reduces people of color to folks who must be taught how to behave and act. If looked at closely, the whole history of racism is a three-way fight between segregationists, assimilationists and antiracism. While segregationist ideas suggest a racial group is permanently inferior, assimilationist ideas suggest a racial group is temporarily inferior. The only truth lies in antiracism which believes that all racial groups are equal to begin with.

Both Black and White dueling consciousness have fashioned their own types of policies. While the White people have generally advocated for both assimilationist and segregationist policies, the Black have been torn between assimilationist and antiracist policies. The only way to be free of this dueling consciousness, therefore, is to be an antiracist and conquer the assimilationist and segregationist consciousness. The White body no longer presents itself as the American body; the Black body no longer strives to be the American body, knowing there is no such thing as the American body, only American bodies, racialized by power.

Chapter 3 - Power

Key Knowledge Pointers

- Race is a power construct of blended differences that lives socially and creates new kinds of power to categorize and judge, elevate and downgrade, include and exclude

- The root of racism lies not in ignorance and hate but rather dwells in the economic, political and cultural self-interest of the racist power

- The racist power creates racist policies out of self-interest and then conceives racist ideas to support these policies

Although as life-changing a power as it is, race is still a mirage. We are what we see ourselves as, whether what we see exists or not. We're also what people see us as, whether what they see exists or not. It's the powerful light of racist power that makes race such an enchanting mirage. But what people see in themselves and others has meaning because it shapes their ideas, behavior and policies.

I still remember the first time I became *racially mature.* I was just a 7-year old boy at the time and was visiting a private Black school with my parents in April 1990. The dueling consciousness of my Black parents did not mind paying for a private school to keep me away from the public schools in my neighborhood where most of the poor Black children studied. It also didn't matter that this new school was a thirty-minute drive out to Long Island twice a day, every weekday, year after year—on top of their hour-long job commutes to Manhattan. I don't pity myself for identifying as Black as such a young age. I still identify as a Black and have no problem with it because recognizing my race has allowed me to clearly see myself historically and politically as being an antiracist. One of the ironies of being an advocate for antiracism is that we must racially identify ourselves in order to understand the privileges and dangers of living inside our own bodies.

Race is a power construct of blended differences that lives socially and creates new kinds of power to categorize and judge, elevate and downgrade, include and exclude. Prince Henry the Navigator is one of the first characters in the history of racist power. Henry had been my middle name as well since my Dad chose it from his family (it was the name of his enslaved great-great grandfather). I changed my middle name to Xolani (meaning peace) later upon learning the history.

Henry sponsored Atlantic voyages to West Africa and created a new form of slavery than what existed previously. His sailors went past the feared "black" hole of Cape Bojador, off Western Sahara, and brought enslaved Africans back to Portugal. But the first person to actually craft racist ideas was Prince Henry's biographer, Gomes de Zurara, who was commissioned by King Afonso V to write a spectacular biography of his uncle's African adventures. In his stories, Zurara describes some captives as "white enough, fair to look upon, and well proportioned," while others as "like mulattoes" and "as black as Ethiops, and so ugly". Besides, although these people didn't have the same skin color and neither did they all belong to a single ethnic group, Zurara merged them into one single group worthy of enslavement. This was done to create a hierarchy which became one of the first racist ideas.

The first use of the term 'race', however, occurred later in a 1481 hunting poem by Jacques de Brézé whereas the first formal definition of the term appeared in a major European dictionary. Later, when Spanish and Portuguese colonizers reached the Americas in the 15th century, they further normalized the increased import of enslaved Africans by calling them "strong for work, the opposite of the natives, so weak who can work only in undemanding tasks". Starting in 1735, Carl Linnaeus formed a racial hierarchy for humans in which he color-coded them as White, Yellow, Red and Black. Each of these races were attributed to one of the four regions of the world and their characteristics described. At the bottom of this hierarchy, Linnaeus placed Homo sapiens afer: "Sluggish, lazy. Black kinky hair. Silky skin. Flat nose. Thick lips. Females with genital flap and elongated breasts. Crafty, slow, careless. Covered by grease. Ruled by caprice". These categories were created for a specific purpose and are still followed by race makers today.

One of the many purposes that these racial categories served was creating a heap of wealth for King Afonso V. The racist ideas purported by the highly obedient Gomes de Zurara were meant to convince the world that the Portuguese slave-trade wasn't done for money but for saving the souls of the people of color. After trading slaves for almost two decades, Alfonso recruited Zurara to defend this very lucrative business of human lives. And thus a group known as the 'Black race' was invented upon which racist ideas were so conveniently hung. It's a vicious cycle: a racist power creates racist policies out of raw self-interest; the racist policies necessitate racist ideas to justify them.

The root problem of racism is not, therefore, ignorance and hate as is widely believed. Instead, it is the economic, political and cultural self-interest of the racist power which then uses intellectual individuals like Zurara to redirect the blame for their era's racial inequities away from those policies and onto people.

Chapter 4 -
Biology

Key Knowledge Pointers

- Biological racism is based on the idea that races are meaningfully different in their biology and that these differences create a hierarchy of value

- These distorted racist beliefs are not only created by misinterpreting the Bible but also science itself

- An antiracist recognizes the reality of biological equality and the racial mirage and strives to end the racism that shapes the mirages

Generalizing the behavior of one White racist individual on their entire race is akin to racist categorizing and is as perilous as generalizing the individual faults of people of color to entire races. It is common for us to remember the race instead of the individual. But an antiracist considers and behaves towards individuals as individuals. Instead of saying, "She acted that way because she is White", an antiracist says, "She acted that way because she is racist".

But my 7-year old self did not understand that.

I don't remember the name of my White third-grade teacher, neither do my parents, but we do remember what she did and blame it all on her race. It was common for the teacher in question to overlook the raised hands of Black students and to punish them unnecessarily. Like my other Black classmates, I used to ignore her behavior. But that became impossible for me when, one day, she deliberately avoided the raised hand of a timid Black girl and engaged a favored White child instead. Unable to control my fury at her ignorance and seeing the spirits of that already shy girl go down, I threw a tantrum at our weekly service held at the chapel in protest. To oppose her actions, I refused to move when the service was over. Unable to process the racist abuse I had witnessed in the class, I wouldn't respond to my teacher's orders or even threats of punishment. My outcry persisted even when the Principal was called and I decided that I wasn't going to move until I had a chance to defend *our* Blackness. Mine and the girl's, who had the same kinky hair, broad nose and thick lips as me. Our White classmates looked foreign to me at that time and I wasn't remotely aware that our apparent differences with them were meaningless to our underlying humanity.

This is the essence of biological racism, drilled into me by adults. It is based on two ideas; that the races are meaningfully different in their biology and that these differences create a hierarchy of value. The dueling racial consciousness in me believed the first idea but rejected the second. Few people realize that they hold biological racist beliefs or that these beliefs are rooted in racist ideas. I grew up hearing how Black people had more natural physical ability, how Black blood was different than White blood and how Black people had natural gifts for improvisation thereby excelling in the fields of rap music, jazz and basketball. I also heard how Black women had naturally large buttocks and how the increased rape of White women could be attributed to Black men having strong sexual desires. Another laughable assertion being that Black people have higher rates of hypertension because only those able to retain high levels of salt survived consuming the salty water of the Atlantic Ocean during the Middle Passage. The irony remains that this hypertension/slavery connection, contrived by a Black researcher, is not based on any lab results rather conceived by a fiction novel from Alex Haley called '*Roots*'.

Even the same Bible that taught me how all humans descended from Adam and Eve argued that a Divine curse resulted in enduring differences amongst the human race. The account of the Biblical Great Flood reveals that one of the three sons of Noah, Ham, saw his father naked as Noah got drunk and fell asleep in his tent. Ham and all his descendants were therefore cursed to be the slave of his brother Shem. Referring to this same story about Noah and his sons, English travel writer George Best endorsed the increased slavery of African people. He declared it *God's will* that Ham's son and "*all his posteritie after him should be so blacke and loathsome that it might remain a spectacle of disobedience to all the world.*"

These distorted racist beliefs are not only created by misinterpreting the Bible but also science itself. When Christopher Columbus discovered the Americas, there were speculations about Native Americans and the Africans descending from 'a different Adam'. Polygenesis - the theory that different races descended from distinct species, was therefore favored by slave traders as it supported the idea that these inferior races could be traded for profit. Although Polygenesis remained a topic of debate throughout the Age of Enlightenment and during the first transatlantic antislavery movement, it governed racial thought in the United States for decades. Ultimately, it prompted the biologist Charles Darwin to say that *"The view which most naturalists entertain, and which I formerly entertained—namely, that each species has been independently created—is erroneous* (as written in The Origin of Species)". Darwin later proposed the theory of natural selection but that was also used to promote biological racist ideas.

Then came the transatlantic eugenics movement which was powered by Darwin's half cousin Francis Galton. Eugenics was meant to quicken the process of natural selection through encouraging reproduction by superior genes and enslaving or killing the inferior ones. These concepts - curse theory, polygenesis, and eugenics - were only disempowered in academics after the outcry against genocide by Nazi Germany in the mid 20th century. However, they still remained strong in common thinking thereby surrounding me when I was a child.

On June 26, 2000 President Bill Clinton made one of the most important scientific announcements when he declared that modern science had confirmed a critical fact of life to be our common humanity. However, Clinton's announcement was soon followed by remarks hinting at the genetic component to human social behavior. This relationship between biology and behavior then became the cradle of biological racism.

Although ethnic ancestry does exist, there is no racial ancestry. Race is assigned to people after they are born. An interesting observation remains that Geneticists found greater genetic diversity between populations in Africa than between Africa and the rest of the world. This makes race just a genetic mirage, one that humanity has organized itself around in extremely real ways.

While the segregationist perceives six biological races and the assimilationist just one, the antiracist recognizes the reality of biological equality and the racial mirage. It focuses on ending the racism that shapes the mirages, not on ignoring the mirages that shape people's lives.

After that encounter with my White teacher and Principal in third grade, Ma explained to me that I must be prepared to deal with the consequences if I wanted to protest against racism. After third grade, I was transferred to St. Joseph's and then to a private Lutheran school in an attempt to better validate my racial identity. Nonetheless, eighth-grade remained a year-long comedy show where everybody would get joked on for something. And some of those jokes hurt the most.

Chapter 5 -
Ethnicity

Key Knowledge Pointers

- Ethnic racism is a powerful collection of racist policies that lead to inequity between racialized ethnic groups

- The core objective to racialize any and all ethnic groups in the country is to create a racial-ethnic hierarchy of value

- Ironically, the main double standard in ethnic racism is to love your position on the ladder of ethnic racism above other groups while hating your position below that of other ethnic groups.

My third-grade nonconformist self had grown a special liking for cruel jokes in the eighth grade. That fall of 1995, a million-man march was held in Washington D.C. and the O.J Simpson trial in Los Angeles concluded with a 'not guilty' verdict. Although the Black adults around me frequently discussed and knew that O.J was guilty, we all wanted him to run free because we also knew that the criminal-justice system wasn't free of guilt either. However, the O.J verdict didn't stop the cruelties of the criminal-justice system. Racist violence against Black people continued and didn't differentiate whether they breathed their first in the United States or abroad.

However, back in that eighth-grade classroom, my African American classmates did differentiate and indulge in ethnic racism. Ethnic racism is essentially a powerful collection of racist policies that lead to inequity between racialized ethnic groups and are substantiated by racist ideas about racialized ethnic groups. We made the nastiest jokes on our classmate 'Kwame' from Ghana and would paraphrase the barbaric and animalistic jokes about Africans to other ethnicities amongst us. Ironically, the point of origin for these racist jokes was the slave trade, which wasn't a joke at all. Ethnic racism is the revival of the script of the slave trader and reawakens the horror stories of racism as we laugh at such jokes.

Ethnic racism originated from the slave trader's demand and supply market where slaves from different ethnic groups were preferred for making better human products. These better slaves were considered better Africans and were sold for twice as much as other 'lower-quality' slaves such as Angolans.

By following the scripts of these slave traders (or planters), me and my friends were originally letting out our anger towards African chiefs who sold their own folks. These African slave traders didn't believe they were selling their own people, rather they thought they were trading people as different to them as the Europeans who were waiting to buy them. It wasn't until perhaps the twentieth century that they became aware that they were all being grouped into a single race.

Being born in the early eighties, I witnessed the surge of immigrants of color coming into the United States first hand. This was a result of the loosening of immigration laws between 1960s through 1990s to amend previous versions of the same law that restricted non-White immigration to the United States. Unlike my parents, some African Americans were wary of this influx of immigrants into the States. These immigrants themselves picked at each other for certain things based on their ethnicities. However, by the early twenty-first century, lawmakers such as U.S. senator Jeff Sessions regretted the growth of the non-White population in the U.S. and began carrying out the Trump administration's anti-Latinx, anti-Arab, and anti-Black immigrant policies geared towards making America White again.

The current administration's retreat to the early twentieth-century's immigration policies is meant to neutralize diversification in America, including the diversity amongst its Black population, all of which are racialized as Black. The core objective to racialize any and all ethnic groups in the country is to create a hierarchy of value. Racist ideas about these racialized ethnic groups are meant to create a racial-ethnic hierarchy, which is essentially a ladder of ethnic racism within the larger body of racism. We can find examples of this ethnic-racial hierarchy throughout the history of the United States; Anglo-Saxons discriminating against Irish Catholics and Jews; Cuban immigrants being privileged over Mexican immigrants etc.

The main double standard in ethnic racism is to love your position on the ladder of ethnic racism above other groups while hating your position below that of other ethnic groups. This leads you to be angered towards racist ideas about your own group while happily consuming racist ideas about another ethnic group. It is failing to recognize that the racist ideas we consume about others came from the same source that serves racist ideas about us all.

When studies came up showing that Black immigrants did so much better than Blacks born in America, it was assumed that it is because Black immigrants are more motivated, hardworking and entrepreneurial than the home grown folk. It was also implied, therefore, that racism doesn't account for the difficulties of native Blacks because the immigrant Blacks fared so well in the same country. However, in reality, Black immigrants' comparisons with Black natives conceals the racial inequities between Black immigrants and non-Black immigrants. An ethnic racist therefore prompts, why are Black immigrants doing better than African Americans? Whereas an ethnic antiracist asks, why are Black immigrants not doing as well as other immigrant groups? With that being said, the main reason why immigrant Blacks do better than the natives is the fact that these folks are uniquely resilient and resourceful, not because of their ethnicity but because of their status as an immigrant. This is called by Sociologists as 'the migrant advantage'. It is another reason why, as such, the racist immigration policies of the current and past administrations have been self-destructive to the country. As with all racism, including ethnic racism, no one wins except the racist powers at the top leaving only confusion and hurt on either side.

Chapter 6 - Body

Key Knowledge Pointers

- The historic stigma attached with the Black body made me afraid of my own Black body as well as that of others around me

- As much as I lived in the fear of Black bodies, I enjoyed many moments of peace and happiness as well

- Regardless of the horrifying image of the Black body, research shows that there is no such thing as a dangerous racial group but dangerous individuals may exist

History tells that violence for White people too often had a Black face. The consequences of this fact have affected Blacks across the span of the American history. They were spoken of in terms like "...ruthless savages" and described as "The poor African has become a fiend, a wild beast, seeking whom he may devour". This is exactly how the racist power has worked i.e. by constructing the Black race biologically and ethnically and then presenting it to the world as "beasts" who must be controlled by force. Today Americans see the Black body as 'large', 'threatening' and 'potentially harmful', even when compared to a similar-sized White body.

After eighth grade, I was enrolled in John Bowne High School in central Queens. Inside this new school, I was surrounded by Black, Latinx and Asian teens. From the time that I was almost eight years old, my parents had inculcated a strong fear of the Black body inside me through their constant fear mongering about Black dealers, killers and robbers. Resultantly, my days inside John Bowne were filled with fear of stepping onto new sneakers and bumping into people, amongst other things. At that time, what could happen to me based on my deepest fears mattered more than what actually happened to me (none of my fears ever materialized!). When I believed that I was being stalked by violence, I was actually being stalked by my own racist ideas. I was as scared of the Black body as the White themselves.

This fear, amongst other things, also numbed my desire to help the victims of violence around me.

Like the time when a teenage boy we nicknamed 'Smurf' started bullying a tiny Indian teen on the school bus. The teen was sitting at the wrong side of the bus and was fixated on the music playing on his new walkman. His eyes were closed and he was unaware of his surroundings which is why he couldn't notice my desperate attempts to direct him to the front of the bus. Other Black and Indian students tried to do the same but with no result. The teen was completely oblivious to our hints and of the danger that was upon him.

And then it happened. Smurf and his crew noticed him and went over to him.

The kid was startled as he finally looked up and saw Smurf and his boys looming over him. I was watching the whole situation with desperation, summoning the courage to employ my natural gift for defusing potentially volatile situations. I had to learn these techniques to avoid the Smurfs of the world as well as the cops who seemed especially fearful of my Black body; for if we weren't able to calm the fears of these violent cops, we were responsible for our own assaults and deaths.

But the kid had already run out of any options to salvage the situation. Before the bus driver could interfere, he was knocked down by Smurf and his crew, who flew from the scene as soon as the bus stopped and the back door opened. You'd think I'll help that poor kid then. But I was still frozen in my seat as some eyes from the crew were still present on the bus.

The Violent Crime Control and Law Enforcement Act of 1993 was introduced by White legislators who were thinking about Black people like Smurf and me. Consequently, it imposed strict measures such as new prisons, capital offenses and the eligibility to be tried as an adult at the age of thirteen. However, unlike the scenario predicted by racist Americans such as Princeton political scientist John J. DiIulio, no 'super-predators' in young Black bodies swarmed the streets. Instead the rate for violent crimes actually started declining. But then crime bills have never corresponded with crime any more than fear corresponds with actual violence. This fear of the unarmed latinx, Arab and Black body is the self-creation of crime entrepreneurs who then make promises to liberate people of these same fears.

The violent acts of Smurf combined with the racist ideas inside my head led me to believe there was more violence among the Black people surrounding me than there actually was. I also believed that this violence defined my own Black body and that I somehow needed to protect myself from my own Blackness. Statistics show that the rate of urban violent crime declined between 1993-2016. Although these figures aren't precise, the idea that directly experienced violence is endemic everywhere or that Black neighborhoods are *worse than war-zones* is complete nonsense.

As much as I lived in the fear of Black bodies, I enjoyed many moments of peace and happiness as well. I understood the dangers of my neighborhood, but I also thought it was safe. Even the neighborhoods and people (like Smurf) that I knew to avoid wasn't because they were Black. Researchers have also found a much stronger and clearer connection between unemployment and violent crime rates than between race and violent crime rates. Consequently, Black neighborhoods with upper and middle-income families had lower violent crime rates than low-income Black neighborhoods.

These findings show that there is no such thing as a dangerous racial group. However, dangerous individuals like Smurf may exist.

Chapter 7 - Culture

Key Knowledge Pointers

- When biological racism was marginalized in the wake of the Nazi holocaust, cultural racism replaced it

- Whoever creates cultural standards puts themselves at the top of the hierarchy, be it Europeans or White Americans

- Being an antiracist implies that one sees all cultures in all their differences as equals and regards cultural differences as just that; *cultural differences*

Basketball was life for me. But on a cool winter day in 1996, me and my teammates at John Bowne's junior-varsity basketball team were informed by our coach that we needed to post two Cs and three Ds to remain on the team. We didn't take it seriously at the time but High School had changed me. It was just my passion for basketball and parental shame that kept me from dropping out and staying home all day like some other teens.

My Ebonics were despised by some Americans in 1996. A look into the history of Ebonics, a formal term coined by psychologist Robert Williams for 'Negro English', shows that enslaved Africans formed new languages in almost every

European colony in the Americas. This practice of language adaptation also includes the Jamaican Patois, Haitian Creole, Brazilian Calunga, and Cubano. The racist power in these countries always demeaned these African languages as 'broken' and 'improper'. Considering that Ebonics had grown from the roots of African languages, just as English was born out of the womb of German, Greek and Latin languages, it is unfair to declare it as 'broken English' when English isn't deemed 'broken German'.

When biological racism was marginalized in the wake of the Nazi holocaust, cultural racism replaced it. Whoever makes the cultural standard makes a cultural hierarchy. These standards and hierarchies then conceive cultural racism. Being an antiracist involves negating cultural standards and eliminating cultural differences. This is unlike the stance of assimilationists like President Theodore Roosevelt and Alexander Crummell who proposed that 'the backward race...' be assimilated and classed the Blacks as fundamentally imitative.

But when it came to the 'Ave', we weren't imitators at all. The Ave was a term we used for the central artery of Southside Queens. On the Ave, it was the mainstream White world that was imitating our culture. We were the gurus of fashion in New York with our fresh gear and even fresher ways to carry it. But not everyone saw us as fresh cultural innovators, including Wall Street Journal columnist Jason Riley, who thought that if we could close the 'civilization gap' the problem of racism could be solved. Mr. Riley was referring to 'cultural racism' when he talked about civilization.

I despised what they called civilization and loved what they termed as dysfunctional; the African American culture created by my ancestors. These ancestors of mine had found creative ways to reinvigorate the culture of their ancestors with what was available to them in the Americas. However, their attempts were regarded as being *"Stripped of his cultural heritage, the Negro's reemergence as a human being was facilitated by his assimilation" of "white civilization"*, by anthropologists, sociologists and scholars alike. What these surface-sighted cultural eyes failed to assess was that there was this 'deep structure of culture' that changed the outward physical forms of how African culture manifested itself in the Americas.

The sound of hip hop was all around us on the Ave. Although hip hop has had the most sophisticated vocabulary of any American musical genre, our elders didn't like us listening to it or memorizing the deviant rhymes. Just like our parents and grandparents, C. Delores Tucker who campaigned against rap music in the mid-1990s contested that "You can't listen to all that language and filth without it affecting you". When we left Queens in 1997 and went South to begin a new life, things changed. Basketball had been my life but when I didn't make into the Stonewall Jackson High School's junior-varsity basketball team, it broke my heart. Nothing remained the same afterwards.

I was an instinctive believer in multiculturalism at that time although I despised the culture of non-urban Blacks and the Southerners I was now surrounded by. This arrogance and snobbery was potentially the reason why people who may have wanted to be friends stayed away from me and rightly so. When we name a group 'Black' or 'White', or even 'Black Southerners' instead of Southerners, we are racializing that group. When such a group is racialized and their culture deemed inferior, we are expressing cultural racism. Judging specific Black racial groups, such as the Southerners, was no different than White New York judging Black New York.

Whoever creates cultural standards puts themselves at the top of the hierarchy, be it Europeans or White Americans. Being an antiracist implies that one sees all cultures in all their differences as equals and regards cultural differences as just that - cultural differences. This realization finally made me respect the African American culture in Northern Virginia.

Chapter 8 - Behavior

Key Knowledge Pointers

- Seeing individuals as responsible for the perceived behavior of racial groups, and vice versa, constitutes behavioral racism

- To be an antiracist is to recognize that there is no 'Black behavior', let alone irresponsible Black behavior

- There is great disagreement between behavioral racists on the cause of Black behavior; some think it's freedom while others contest it's slavery that caused it

I was an irresponsible student in high school. In spite of finally making friends after almost two years of isolation, I failed to live up to my academic potential. It makes antiracist sense to discuss the personal irresponsibility of individuals like me within all races. When President Bill Clinton argued in 1995 that *"It isn't racist for Whites to say they don't understand why people put up with gangs on the corner or in the projects or with drugs being sold in the schools or in the open"*, he was pointing to personal irresponsibility and I get that. What I fail to understand, however, is how then the academic incompetency of some of my White friends didn't somehow defamed their race.

My personal irresponsibility issues were caused as well as aggravated by the racism surrounding me. Granted, I could have conquered that racism if I tried harder. But it is unreasonable to expect another unexceptional Black person to survive the racist attacks they have to endure each day and be extraordinary regardless. That is purely racist in itself. It is one of the fundamental values of racism to bestow success on even the most unexceptional Whites while reserving just a modicum of moderate success for extraordinary Black individuals.

It is true that individual behaviors can shape the success of individuals but it is also a fact that policies determine the success of groups. And it is the racist power that creates policies that cause racial inequities. Seeing individuals as responsible for the perceived behavior of racial groups, and vice versa, constitutes behavioral racism. The progressive Americans who had discarded ethnic, bodily and cultural racism by the mid-1990s were still convinced by the idea of behavioral racism.

To be an antiracist is to recognize that there is no 'Black behavior', let alone irresponsible Black behavior. That is because there is no scientific evidence behind Black behavioral traits. Antiracism also involves identifying the differences between the idea of a culture from the idea of a behavior. Culture defines a group tradition that a particular racial group might share but that is not shared among all individuals in that racial group or among all racial groups. Behavior defines the inherent human traits and potential that everyone shares. For instance, laziness and intelligence are two common human traits, yet these aren't the same among racialized cultural groups.

The behavioral racists don't even agree among themselves. Some proslavery theorists suggest it is freedom that caused the Black behavior whereas other antislavery enthusiasts conclude that it is slavery that is the root of these behavioral issues. The latest tangent in this context is known as post-traumatic slave syndrome (PTSS). This claims that the Black behavior, in large, is the result of trans-generational adaptations to a history of slavery. There is no doubt that Black individuals have suffered trauma from slavery and ongoing oppression. However, there is very little difference between an antiracist stating the Blacks have suffered trauma and a racist declaring Blacks as traumatized people. Later in the twentieth century, social scientists swapped slavery with segregation and discrimination as the driver for Black behavior but the ugliness of behavioral racism remained the same.

This behavioral racism not only affected teenagers like me externally but also internally as the older generations in our families generalized our personal failings as the failure of our entire race. But there were exceptions, and my parents were one of them. Regardless of my academic incompetence, they did not give up on me and kept trying. However, their efforts only pulled me down further as I saw students around me aspiring for higher goals while I struggled to shape myself according to other people's perceptions about me. This led to me internalizing these academic struggles as some sort of a failure in the overall Black behavior.

I thought of myself as a fool as I compared my academic performance to my White or Asian classmates. It wasn't until my senior year at college that I realized I was wrong in thinking that I was a fool. When earlier I thought that standardized tests were an effective measurement of a student's intelligence, I now realized that they were one of the most effective racist policies to degrade and exclude Black minds. This is because the scores of these tests very objectively imply that discrepancies in academic achievement reflect discrepancies in intelligence among racial groups. When, in fact, the only difference lies in a student's economic privilege and their awareness about the highly-priced prep courses that can train them to score high in such tests.

The widely accepted idea of an 'academic-achievement gap' is another method of reinforcing the inferiority of Black intellect. In reality, it is the 'opportunity gap' that has resulted in the underperformance of Black and Latinx students.

After giving that racist speech I talked about earlier in the book in 1999, I decided to attend Florida A&M University which was the biggest HBCU (historically Black college and university) in the country. However, it wasn't just the desire to be around Black excellence that motivated my decision to go to Florida A&M University (FAMU) but a deep underlying eagerness to get away from the misbehaving Black people around me.

Chapter 9 – Color

Key Knowledge Pointers

- The post-racial beauty ideal is the latest form of Colorism which is a collection of racist policies that cause inequities between Light and Dark people

- Antiracism focuses on color lines as much as racial lines because they create inequities 'within' races, in addition to 'between' races

- To be an antiracist isn't to reverse beauty standards rather to eliminate them entirely

The cornrowed hair and 'honey' contact lens that I flaunted in college intertwined the assimilationist and antiracist ideas of my dueling consciousness. I didn't care that my cornrows would be judged by racists but I also strived to look White with my one-shade-lighter-than-usual hazel contacts. I wanted to be Black but without looking Black. The post-racial beauty ideal 'lightness', which portrayed an image with lighter skin and eyes, straighter hair, thinner noses, and semi-thick lips and buttocks, was guiding me. It was perceived as biracial or racially ambiguous and was the latest form of 'Colorism' which is a collection of racist policies that cause inequities between Light people and Dark people. These inequities are then rationalized by racist and assimilationist ideas about Light and Dark people that encourage transforming into something closer to the White body.

Antiracism focuses on color lines as much as racial lines because they create inequities 'within' races, in addition to 'between' races. This is illustrated in Dark Black students getting lower GPAs than lighter Black students and Light Black men being preferred over Dark Black men by employers regardless of qualifications. Similarly, Dark African Americans receive tougher prison sentences than their Lighter counterparts. These inequities between Light and Dark African Americans can be as wide as inequities between Black and White Americans.

My first date at university was a Light-skinned woman. I abruptly broke off with her when I noticed my friends belittling her Dark skinned roommate while admiring her light skin. From that point on, I pledged to date Dark women in future only and resented anyone, including my friends, who didn't approve of my disposition. I didn't realize at that time that I was just turning the color hierarchy upside down. But it still remained there.

It is ironic that Black people think of themselves as the judge and standard for Blackness while aspiring to be White simultaneously. To maintain the purity of their individual racial groups, White, Black and Light people have historically followed certain rules. While White people have adopted the one-drop rule (one drop of Black blood makes you Black), Black people have observed the two-drop rule (two drops of White blood make you less Black) whereas Light people employ the three-drop rule (three drops of Black blood mean you're too Dark). These rules are merely mirages, just like the races themselves.

To be an antiracist isn't to reverse beauty standards, rather it is to eliminate them entirely. It is to diversify our standards of beauty to include all skin colors, facial features and body structures and to enhance our natural beauty instead of altering it.

Colorism is also evident in the slave trader's philosophy whereby a Light body was considered more suitable for skilled tasks than a Black one which was deemed more fit for physical work. Some other slave traders, however, considered Lighter folks or 'mulatto' less perfect than Blacks although they secretly preferred Lighter women as smarter, kinder, gentler, and more beautiful than Dark women.

After emancipation in 1865, Light people barred Dark people from their communities just like White folks built high walls of segregation to keep the Black people out. These Light people came out wealthier in the post-slavery period than their Dark counterparts and barred them from their churches, parties, organizations and HBCUs. However, they were still segregated from Whiteness. The interracial intercourse of White human and the 'Black beast' was considered a heinous sin and rebellious Light men were being hanged for the rape of White women. It was the Sociologist Edward Byron Reuter who made Light people into a sort of racial middle class, with White people above them and the Blacks below. He defended them from eugenicists and from Dark people who questioned their colorism.

In 1920, Sociologist W.E.B. Du Bois declared that the existence of colorism was rejected by the Negro, but that was far from the truth. He changed his mind in the 1930s replacing Marcus Garvey, a Dark activist, as the chief antiracist critic of The National Association for the Advancement of Colored People (NAACP). In the post WWI era, it became fashionable for Black men and women to straighten their hair and to use skin-lightening products. But by the early 1970s, Black power activists inspired by Malcolm X and Angela Davis were returning to their original self, including my parents.

However by the late 1970s, the Light ideal came back, and this time with a vengeance. From the 1980s onwards, Light children fared much better than Dark ones, the demand for fairness products skyrocketed and skin-bleaching treatments were popularized by celebrities such as Michael Jackson. Although White people have their own addictions with 'skin tanning', they look down upon the Blacks bleaching their skin as if there is really that much difference between the two. Surveys show that people consider tanned skin—the replica color of Light people—more attractive than naturally pale skin and Dark skin.

To be an antiracist is to advocate for policies that lead to equity between Light people and Dark people and that are supported by antiracist ideas about Light and Dark people.

Chapter 10 - White

Key Knowledge Pointers

- Delving into White history to justify my hatred for White people, I noticed that it was strangely similar to that of what Black people taught me in White schools

- To be an antiracist is to never mistake the hate for White racism for the hate of White people. It is to know that there are antiracist Whites as well as racist non-Whites

- In the end, hating White people only becomes hating Black people and hating Black people becomes hating White people

Anti-Black racist ideas covered my eyes like those hazel contacts that I started wearing after arriving at FAMU. On the evening of November 7th, 2000, we were gathered in the television room to watch the election results come through. We had deliberately voted against the racist brother of Jeb Bush and rejoiced when Al Gore's win was finally announced. However, the arrival of the next day brought with it a recount held under the supervision of Jeb Bush's appointees that turned the tables by just 537 votes.

In the weeks that followed, I heard the stories of FAMU students and their families back home not being able to vote. There were Black citizens that never received their registration cards, or had their voting locations changed or were told that they could not vote as convicted felons when some of them weren't convicted felons at all. Reporters and campaign officials alike focused on votes that weren't counted or were counted the wrong way instead of the people who weren't allowed to vote in the first place. The only explanation for whatever's going on was racism, but I couldn't recognize it at first.

Assembling the courage I lacked, my fellow students at FAMU operated a silent march and sit-in on November 9th, 2000. Back at the campus, we launched a witch hunt against those who didn't vote and shamed them. I foolishly joined the hunt, ignorant of the fact that a significant number of Black people indeed turned out to vote but were sent home or their votes spoiled. My anti-Black racist ideas forced me to blame the victim for their own victimization. As the recount was halted by the U.S Supreme Court and Gore admitted his defeat, I started hating White people.

To justify my hatred for White people, I began delving into history. In "The Making of Devil," a chapter in Elijah Muhammad's "*Message to the Blackman in America*", I read that White people were originally created by a wicked scientist Yakub who was exiled to an island. Yakub vowed to create a devil race in vengeance, therefore producing blond, pale-skinned and cold-blue-eyed savages by selective breeding of the Black race on the island. Upon invading the mainland, these White people created chaos which is why they were chained by the Black authorities and sent to the prison caves of Europe. When Moses came, he lifted these folks out of these caves and taught them civilization.

This history of White people was strangely similar to that of Black people taught to me in White schools. It is so similar that it could be considered the racist history of Black people in Whiteface. I was mesmerized the first time I read this story and felt great anger towards all the Whites who had berated me in life. But my attention was focused on those that had derailed the Florida elections of 2000.

Like me, a young Black prisoner in 1948 also considered White man to be the devil. An unfair prison sentence and grave injustices towards his family turned this young man into Malcolm Little and later Malcolm X. After leaving the prison in 1952, Malcolm X began growing Elijah Muhammad's Nation of Islam (NOI). However in 1964, he openly rejected Elijah Muhammad's racist philosophies and admitted that he was the only one to be blamed for his foolishness in following Elijah. Malcolm X understood that Black people can be racist towards White people, a notion that many of his followers are unaware of. Saying something is wrong with the White people is a racist idea as well. The only thing wrong with White people is when they embrace racist ideas and policies and then deny their ideas and policies are racist. This must not overlook the fact that these White people have massacred, enslaved and colonized millions of Black people. It simply implies that their ransacking is not rooted in their genes or culture.

To be an antiracist is to never mistake the hate for White racism for the hate of White people. It is to know that there are antiracist Whites as well as racist non-Whites. We must also understand the difference between racist powers aka policymakers and White people. Of course, ordinary White people benefit from racist policies, but not as much as the racist power themselves or as the super-rich White man. The racist ideas which the racist power uses to justify their racist policies also harm the White people by convincing them that it is somehow their personal failure when they're unable to succeed and has nothing to do with policies.

Racist power also manipulates White people by telling them that any equalizing policies are in fact anti-White. These claims of anti-white racism in response to antiracism are as old as civil rights. The ordinary White racist is a soldier of the racist power, declaring all policies unaccommodated for Whites as racist. This is primarily why people of color are anti-White racists, it is hate produced by hate. However, going after White people instead of the racist power only harms Black lives as it diverts their attention from the racist policies. In the end, hating White people only becomes hating Black people.

And in the end, hating Black people becomes hating White people.

My hatred for White people carried into my sophomore year. I kept digging into history to find the biological theories that would justify White evil such as Frances Cress Welsing's 'color confrontation theory' and Cheikh Anta Diop's 'two-cradle theory'. My attempts to figure out White people so *we Blacks knew what we're dealing with* (as I often said to my roommate Clarence), took me to a public writing career on race. It all started with a column in FAMU's student newspaper which made great waves in Tallahassee.

And as I was summoned into the office of the Tallahassee Democrat's editor, I knew something was going to end that day.

Chapter 11 - Black

Key Knowledge Pointers

- Racializing the negative behaviors of some Black people and attaching criminality to niggers doesn't make us much different to White racists

- Believing that people of color can't be racists because they lack power frees people of color from charges of racism and production of racist policies

- Black people can be racists because they do have power, albeit limited

While 'nigga' was a charming term used by hip-hop artists, 'nigger' remained a disdainful word in the Black mind. The racial construct of '*them niggers*' was immensely popularized by the comedian Chris Rock in his 1996 HBO special *Bring the Pain*. As we laughed at Chris Rock's jokes calling niggers unequal to the Black man and thereby creating hierarchies amongst ourselves, we were simultaneously (and hypocritically) enraged when the Whites called us all niggers.

We weren't treating the negative attributes of some Black people as individual characteristics and consequently failed to put them into an interracial group. Rather, we racialized their negative behaviors and attached criminality to niggers. This didn't make us much different to the White racists. After doing all of this as Black racists, we identified ourselves as 'not-racist' like a White racist would. At that time, we felt a tremendous antiracist pride in Black excellence and a tremendously racist shame in being connected to '*them niggers*'. In this context, we recognized the impact of the racist policies we were facing but didn't acknowledge the racist policies '*them niggers*' had to endure. At that time, our anti-Black racist ideas were the real Black on Black crime.

From 2003 onwards, more Black people considered reasons other than racism to explain persistent racial inequities. This was most likely due to the internalizing of racist ideas which led these Black folks to believe that racism wasn't the reason Blacks had poor jobs and housing. However, this view changed significantly by 2017 when 59% of Black people expressed racism to be the main reason Blacks couldn't succeed. Sadly, one third of the Black population still blamed Blacks for their own sufferings.

As I sat in the the office of the Tallahassee Democrat's editor and heard his remarks about the niggers, I couldn't help but face the truth that he was saying what I was thinking the whole time. This made me feel enraged although we weren't much different when it came to our criticism for Black people. Putting two and two together that day, I realized my own racist tendencies. Every time I said something was wrong with the

Blacks, I was separating myself from them and was being a racist in doing so.

I believed that Blacks, Latinx, Asians, Middle Easterners, and Natives couldn't be racists because they lacked power. This 'powerless defense' originally rose as an armor against White racists' opposition of the antiracist policies. It acts as a shield, protecting people of color in powerful positions from acting on the premise of a lack of power, when they can actually do the work of antiracism. It also frees people of color from charges of racism and production of racist policies. It underestimates Black people and expands the already growing influence of White power.

The truth is that Black people can be racist because they do have *limited* power, with emphasis being on the word 'limited'. White power doesn't control the U.S. *absolutely* because it doesn't have complete control over all levels of powers, policies, policy managers and minds. Accepting that we have no power will ultimately rob us of any power to resist for real.

The state-of-the-art racist work of suppressing Black votes for Bush's reelection by Ohio's ambitious Black Secretary of State, Ken Blackwell, is a clear example of Black power in action. According to the theory that Black people can't be racist because they lack power, Blackwell didn't have the power to suppress Black votes, but he did that anyway. It is the widespread acceptance of the powerless defense that lets Black on Black criminals like Ken Blackwell get away with their racism. To say Black people can't be racist is to say all Black people are being antiracist at all times. My own story tells me otherwise. History agrees.

One of the most well-organized slave revolts in American history was spoiled by a Black slave called Peter Prioleau. This Black slave had no intentions to leave his master and instead used his power to spoil the revolt. He resembled William Hannibal Thomas, another Black man, who wanted to be accepted amongst the Whites so he declared his own race an *'intrinsically inferior type of humanity'*. These Black on Black criminals repeatedly betrayed their own in the twentieth century. Even the diversification of the police force in the 1960s didn't stop them. Anti-Black racist ideas existed among a significant minority of Black policemen and their brutality against Black people continued. The situation was further exacerbated by Black people who bombarded politicians and police officers with their racist fears of *Black* criminals as opposed to criminals in general. This fueled the rise of mass incarceration, and until the 1980s, had taken the form of a housing crisis made worse as well as a rise in employment discrimination against Blacks. All being the doings of Black on Black criminals who used their power, no matter how limited, in racist ways.

As that meeting with the Tallahassee Democrat's editor concluded with me taking my race column in *Famuan* down, my confusion ended as well. For the first time, I started to see that the battle was indeed between racists and antiracists instead of being among Blacks, Whites and *'them niggers'*.

Chapter 12 -
Class

- Saying 'Poor Blacks' essentially combines racist and elitist ideas. This ideological intersection creates class racism

- To be an antiracist is to recognize that the root cause of economic disparities among people would be policies, not those people themselves

- To be an antiracist is to recognize that neither poor Blacks nor elite ones truly depict the Black people

Starting graduate school in African American studies at Temple University was very exciting for me. However, it led me to move to the most dangerous neighborhoods of Philadelphia. The area was frivolously called 'the ghetto'. Instead of bringing to mind the racist policies that led to White people fleeing these neighborhoods and the Black folks herein being abandoned, the term described unrespectable Black behavior. Blacks in the ghetto were considered 'pathological' which implies being extreme in a way that is different from the norm. But who, then, was the norm?

Poor Blacks in the *ghetto* were racial groups at the intersection of race and class. To say that poor people are lazy is an elitist idea whereas it is a racist idea to proclaim that Black people are lazy. Saying 'Poor Blacks' essentially combines racist and elitist ideas. This ideological intersection creates class racism. Policies exploiting Black poor people, therefore, are a policy intersection of class racism. To be an antiracist is to recognize that the root cause of economic disparities among people is policies, not those people themselves. It is to understand that the political and economic conditions in poor Black neighborhoods are pathological, not the people themselves.

People within a 'Culture of poverty', a term introduced by anthropologist Oscar Lewis, are described as marginal people who know only their own troubles, their own local conditions, their own neighborhood, their own way of life. White racists refer to this as a cultural problem and use it to keep the hidden hand of racism, hidden. According to the oppression-inferiority thesis, poverty was making the Black people inferior and welfare was the primary culprit for this poverty. Although the conservative version of this theory considered welfare for Black people to be the true oppressor, it quite conveniently left welfare for White upper- and middle-income people out of discussion. Even Kenneth Clark's relentless work on exposing racist policies that made the dark ghetto were infused with racial-class hierarchy. Clark positioned the Black poor as inferior in comparison to Black elites like himself and considered the Black poor less stable than the White poor. During his campaign in 2008, former President Obama made a similar case. All of this pigeonholed the Black poor into hopelessness and defeat, with little evidence to support this stereotype.

For ages, racist Blacks and poor Whites alike have increased their sense of self on the basis of the idea that they aren't them niggers, at least. I had come a long way by 2005, and by then, the term 'Dark' had married 'Ghetto'. I didn't care if people called my new home a ghetto, which had become as much an adjective as a noun by then. I also didn't know capitalism at the time but it's impossible to know racism without understanding its intersection with capitalism.

The transatlantic slave trade of African people gave birth to conjoined twins-capitalism and racism. These newborns were then adopted and raised by Spain, which was the primary customer of the Portuguese slave traders. Grown into adolescence by Holland, France and England as they beat each other for authority within the slave trade, these twins entered adulthood through Native, Black, Asian and White slavery and forced labor in the Americas. The twins got weak in the twentieth century but struggle to stay alive as their own offsprings, namely inequality, war, and climate change threatened to kill them. The twenty-first century saw the lifework of these evil twins come to fruition in the form of poverty, unemployment and wealth differences.

The inequities caused by racism and capitalism are not only limited to America. They also spread to Africa where it is forecasted that nearly nine in ten extremely poor people will live in Sub-Saharan Africa by 2030. Attributing these inequities solely to capitalism is as faulty as attributing them entirely to racism. Similarly, these inequities cannot be eliminated through only eliminating racism or capitalism.

Socialist and communist spaces are not automatically antiracist. By asking people of color to leave their antiracism at the door, these socialists and communists seem unfamiliar with Karl Marx's (their ideological guide) viewpoint who recognized the birth of the conjoined twins in his writings. After extensively reading the work of Karl Marx and recognizing government's racism for Black workers, W.E.B. Du Bois conceived the idea of an antiracist anticapitalism. An antiracist anticapitalist would not only seal the horizontal fissures of class but also enclose the vertical fissures of race. After being driven underground in the 1950s and then reemerging in the 1960s, these antiracist anticapitalists are resurfacing again in the twenty-first century.

These two conjoined twins-capitalism and racism-are two sides of the same destructive body. The idea of capitalism, as defined by some conservative defenders, is as comical as the White-

Supremacist idea that calling something racist is the primary form of racism; It has no historical or material reality.

I had come to my new neighborhood in an attempt to study Black people, thinking that poor Black people would be the best representatives of their culture. In reality, I was being a racist by playing Black people cheap as humans. To be an antiracist is to recognize that neither poor Blacks nor elite ones truly depict the Black people. But at that time I considered poor Blacks as both the bottom and foundation of Blackness and Black middle-class as 'inferior'. These racist ideas were, of course, wrong.

Chapter 13 - Space

Key Knowledge Pointers

- Violence and non-violence exists in all spaces, no matter how poor or rich, Black or non-Black

- Policies of space racism are justified through creating a racial hierarchy of space and deploy more resources to White spaces than to Black ones

- An antiracist strategy requires open and equal access to all public accommodations, all integrated White spaces, Middle Eastern spaces, Black spaces, Latinx spaces, Native spaces, and Asian spaces that are as equally resourced as they are culturally different

Our African American studies space at Temple University was called *Black space*. After all, it was governed by Black thoughts, bodies, cultures, and histories. However, the White space at the university wasn't labelled like us. I enrolled at the African American studies doctoral program at Temple which was created by Professor Molefi Kete Asante to help Black people reject seeing everything from a *European perspective*.

When an intellectually confident and fearless Professor Ama Mazama (who was also the right-hand woman of Asante) lectured in my first course that it was impossible to be objective, I was intrigued. I asked her that if we can't be objective then what should we strive to be? Her reply was simple, "Just tell the truth. That's what we should strive to do. Tell the truth."

Racist Whites on the campus showed concern about the 'ghetto' walking around them. They couldn't understand why we worried about safeguarding our Black space when they were equally protective of their White space. They called Black studies 'ghetto', just like my neighborhood, and insisted that we made this ghetto ourselves.

The stigmatization of Black neighborhoods as places of homicides and violence is extremely racist and the most misleading of racist ideas. This is not to imply that Black spaces or White spaces are more or less violent. It's simply acknowledging that violence and non-violence exists in all spaces, no matter how poor or rich, Black or non-Black. And no matter the effect of the conjoined twins-capitalism and racism. Just like the racist power racializes people, it racializes spaces. A space is racialized when a racial group is known to either govern the space or make up a clear majority in the space. Policies of space racism are justified through creating a racial hierarchy of space and deploy more resources to White spaces than to Black ones.

Our graduate program classmates were mostly Black who had come into Philadelphia from other Black colleges and universities. Most of them were extremely proud of their schools but nobody hated their HBCU more than the only other FAMU alum in our graduate program-Nashay. Nashay cited one horrible error of one person in one office to condemn our entire university. But I had heard it all before like my uncle who contested that HBCUs don't represent the real world. When people contend that Black spaces do not represent reality, they are speaking from the White perspective. They are implying that the real American world is White. Being an antiracist is to recognize that there is no 'real world' but 'real worlds' with multiple worldviews. Comparing HBCUs with White colleges (HCWUs) is unfair owing to the disproportionate resource allocation between the two. Nashay's story made me angry at her, but more with myself as I realized that I was guilty of devaluing the very soil that made me a plant.

The antiracist desire to separate from racists is different from the segregationist desire to separate from "inferior" Blacks. It is also different from the integrationist strategy which expects Black bodies to heal in proximity to Whites who haven't yet stopped fighting them. When Black people gather in their own spaces to separate themselves from racism, the integrationists see these as spaces of White hate. They equate spaces for the survival of Black bodies with spaces for the survival of White supremacy and use segregation and separation interchangeably. The lines between segregation and separation are further blurred by segregationists who called their policies 'separate but equal', when these actually redirected resources to White spaces. In the *Brown v. Board of Education* case in 1954, separation was considered to be inherently unequal. But what actually made the public schools unequal was the unequal distribution of resources, not merely separation.

In the *Brown* decision, the court also augmented the legitimacy of integrated White spaces which included some non-Whites and weren't completely dominated by White people and cultures. This integrated White space was deemed the ideal space to develop inferior non-Whites. As part of this integration process, it was believed that the experience of an integrated situation made all the difference in the lives of Black children. Even the "academic-achievement gap" closed with the integration of White schools. But what if the scoring gap closed because more Black students, as part of integration with White schools, started receiving the same education and test prep?

An antiracist strategy requires open and equal access to all public accommodations, all integrated White spaces, Middle Eastern spaces, Black spaces, Latinx spaces, Native spaces, and Asian spaces that are as equally resourced as they are culturally different. It combines an elimination of all barriers to all racialized spaces with a form of integration and social solidarity. It exists to equate and nurture cultural differences and challenge the racist policies that produce resource inequity.

Chapter 14 - Gender

Key Knowledge Pointers

- Saying someone is a Black woman is essentially identifying a race-gender; Black (race) and Woman (gender). When a policy produces inequities between race-genders, it is known as gendered racism

- To be an antiracist is to reject not only the hierarchy of races but of race-genders

- Gender racism hasn't only been at the heart of the oppression against Black women but has also, in some cases, affected White women

- All racial groups are a collection of intersectional identities differentiated by gender, sexuality, class, ethnicity, skin color, nationality, and culture

Arriving at Temple University as a sexist and homophobe, Kaila and Yaba were two women I least expected to befriend. Kaila knew no self-censoring and openly exhibited her lesbian feminism whereas Yaba had encyclopedic knowledge of the Black people. I always felt overwhelmed around them as I laughed hysterically at their jokes or felt in awe of their insights.

I had grown up with my parents' ideas of gender and equality. I wasn't exactly raised to be a Black patriarch but I became one because I wasn't taught how to be a feminist. Initially, both genders were involved in a low-level war where the Black males dominated and critiqued the Black females. However, the dynamics of this conflict changed considerably when a 1965 report by assistant secretary of labor, Daniel Patrick Moynihan, claimed that twice as many Black families were headed by Black females than White ones. The report called for empowering Black men and caused racist patriarchs all around to demand submission of Black women in order to uplift the race. Racism was portrayed as being 'clearly' focused on the Black male and 'sexual rejection of the racial minority' considered a major reason for the unfulfilment of an integrated American society.

The Black Power movement that emerged after the Moynihan report therefore became a struggle for Black men against White men for Black power over Black women. Although this power struggle was almost non-existent in my household, my parents couldn't help but join the interracial force policing the sexuality of young Black mothers. They were amongst a vast majority of liberals and conservatives horrified by more Black children being raised in single parent-households. They considered sexual irresponsibility and pathologizing poverty, amongst other things, as reasons for the increasing number of Black babies being born into single-parent households. But they were wrong at so many levels and were disconnected from the racial reality.

My Ma had been rethinking Christian sexism for some time which is why she openly resisted the traditional wedding vows about '*obeying*' her husband. After my parents wed in 1976, the 'Black feminist movement' had burst through the doors of the sexist Christian churches. These Black feminists fought sexism in Black spaces and racism in women's spaces and developed their own spaces to liberate Black women. Antiracist queer people, withstanding homophobia in Black spaces and racism in queer spaces, had built their own spaces as well which doubled down as antiracist feminist spaces. Black feminists, starting from Maria Stewart and Sojourner Truth to Nikki Giovanni and Alice Walker, identified, considered, and prioritized the oppression Black females faced. In 1991, Black feminist scholars built on the work of their predecessors by introducing specific terminology that named the oppression facing Black women. It was the same time that Afro-Dutch scholar Philomena Essed talked about the intersection between sexism and racism, referring to it as a hybrid phenomenon termed by her as '*gendered racism*'.

Just like sexist policies produce inequity between men and women, racist policies produce inequities between racial groups. When we identify someone as a Black woman, we are essentially identifying a race-gender; Black (race) and Woman (gender). When a policy produces inequities between race-genders, it is known as *gendered racism*. To be an antiracist is to reject not only the hierarchy of races but of race-genders whereas to be feminist is to reject not only the hierarchy of genders but also of race-genders. In this context, being a true

70

antiracist or feminist is the same; you cannot be one without being the other.

Gender racism hasn't only been at the heart of the oppression against Black women but has also, in some cases, affected White women. It has produced an image of a perfect woman to be that of the weak White woman, a notion which went against Hilary Clinton running for Presidency in 2016. Male resistance to feminism has been similarly destructive as gender racism also affects Black men in some cases. For instance, reinforcing the sexist notion of 'real' men as strong and the racist notion of Black men as 'not really men' has produced the image of a weak Black man who is inferior to their White counterpart. The hyper dangerous Black man image was created in a similar manner; through a combination of the sexist notion that women are naturally weak and the racist notion that Black people are more dangerous than Whites.

All racial groups are a collection of intersectional identities differentiated by gender, sexuality, class, ethnicity, skin color, nationality, and culture. The traditional feminists and antiracists fail to recognize this intersectionality which is essential for all humankind. Since Black women were the first to recognize these intersectional differences, a theory for Black women essentially becomes a theory for humanity. This is what these Black feminists have been saying from the beginning; when humanity becomes serious about the freedom of Black women, it becomes serious about the freedom of humanity.

Chapter 15 - Sexuality

Key Knowledge Pointers

- Race-sexualities are racial groups at the intersection of race and sexuality and queer racism produces inequities between the race-sexualities

- The way men and women traditionally behave isn't tied to their biology at all

- Kaila and Yaba were my first role models of Black feminism, queer antiracism and antiracist feminism, who transformed my curiosity into a desire to be a gender antiracist

Race-sexualities are racial groups at the intersection of race and sexuality. For instance, Latinx (race) homosexuals (sexuality) are a race-sexuality. Just like a homophobic policy results into inequities between heterosexuals and homosexuals and a racist policy drives inequities between racial groups, queer racism produces inequities between the race-sexualities.

Homophobia and racism have intersected for ages. Physicians like Havelock Ellis used the anatomy of Black women's bodies to prove the biological differences between sexualities.

Homophobic physicians like him proclaimed that Black lesbians would almost always have a more prominent clitoris. First the racist ideas that Black people are more hypersexual than Whites and then the homophobic ideas suggesting queer people are more hypersexual than heterosexuals, converge to produce queer racism.

My lifelong struggle against the homophobia of my upbringing began when I found out that my best friend at Temple, Weckea, was gay. Weckea didn't tell me about his homosexuality himself which I attributed to the fact that he had somehow sensed my homophobia. I used to think that Black gay men had unprotected sex all the time so a greater number of them contracted HIV than White gay men. I also presumed that gay men had a feminine streak to them which is why all those Black gay men in my modeling troupe in FAMU pinged my "gaydar". But I was so wrong in thinking all of this. Unlike what I thought, Black gay men like Weckea were more masculinity instead of femininity and preferred gay men who performed femininity for partners. Black gay men were also less likely to have unprotected sex so didn't contract HIV as much as White gay men.

I was unaware that the way men and women traditionally behaved wasn't tied to their biology at all. With the help of feminists like Kaila and Yaba, I was learning that men can authentically perform femininity as effectively as women can authentically perform masculinity. In doing so, these men and women are just being who they are without worrying about society's gender conventions.

By not disclosing his sexuality to me, Weckea was probably protecting himself and our friendship. But I had to choose between homophobia and Wackea, so I selected the latter. In doing so, I had chosen to be a queer antiracist which involves equating all race-sexualities and striving to eliminate the differences between them. One cannot become an antiracist if they are homophobic or transphobic. To be a queer antiracist is to see homophobia, racism, and queer racism, not the queer person and certainly not the queer space, as the problem.

The presence of Kaila and Yaba was unmistakable and memorable wherever they went. They taught me that I cannot consider myself a defender of the Black race if I wasn't defending Black women and Black queers. Whenever these two encountered homophobic and patriarchal ideas at a department event, they would come after it. I called these defenses 'attacks' as I felt my own gender and queer racism being assaulted and I didn't want to be a prey to their savage defence.

Intrigued by their brilliance and constructive criticism, I read up on every author they mentioned publicly and privately to me. Kaila and Yaba did me a favor by not letting me run away from them when I felt overwhelmed by their knowledge and insights. Instead, they engaged me in small talk and then long talk with them. Their jokes and attacks considered no gender or sexuality and they were particularly hard on patriarchal White women - those supporting patriarchal White men. The queer Black feminism of these two Black women helped me first separate homophobic from heterosexual, sexist from men and feminist from women and then later racist from White people and antiracist from Black people.

Kaila and Yaba were my first role models of Black feminism, queer antiracism and antiracist feminism, who transformed my curiosity into a desire to be a gender antiracist, a queer antiracist and to not fail ALL Black people.

Chapter 16 - Failure

Key Knowledge Pointers

- The wrongful policies of moral, educational and uplift suasion cause antiracist solutions to fail and racism to continue living amongst us

- Our antiracist power is anything but flexible and is too often bound by ideologies that are in turn bound by failed strategies of racial change

- To be an antiracist is to let me be myself without any obligation to act on behalf of my race

Racism lives because antiracist solutions fail. And these solutions fail because of failed racial ideologies and seeing race as a social construct, racial history as a single march, and racial problems as being rooted in hate and ignorance. In reality, race is a power construct, racist history must've been a fight for antiracism whereas racial problems must be thought of as rooted in power self-interests. Despite constant failure, the popularity of strategies to combat racism remains intact because they are based on the most popular racial ideologies. However, the devastation invoked by repetitive failure of the approach against racism keeps multiplying over time.

I grew up with the burden all Black bodies had to bear, i.e. moral, educational and uplift suasion. These implied that I had to be perfect before both White people and Black people (who were judging if I was representing my race well), that my good behavior would somehow persuade the White racism away and that my own success would uplift my race. Like me, my date Sadiqa had also been taught the same. One day, a conversation sparked between me and Sadiqa upon witnessing some extremely inappropriate behavior from a White man in a restaurant. That day, we shared a few critical remarks about uplift suasion for the first time. However, this discussion continued afterwards and put us on a path to freedom from ideologies like uplift suasion. Years later, I realized that if someone judges my behavior as representative of my race then that's their problem, not mine.

To be an antiracist is to let me be myself without any obligation to act on behalf of my race. But abolitionists like William Lloyd Garrison would disagree. Moral, educational and uplift suasion focused on persuading White people but what if persuading an average White person is not persuading the White policymakers? These strategies relied on appealing to the White racist's moral conscience but what if they had no moral conscience in the first place? What if the real drivers of racist policies are the self-interests of the policymakers and not hate or ignorance?

The core of the problem of race has always been the problem of power, not immorality or ignorance. In 1934, W.E.B. Du Bois critically assessed the strategy of educational suasion just like Garrison had critically assessed moral suasion before him. He called for Black people to focus on accumulating power instead. However, Du Bois' preachings were opposed by Gunnar Myrdal who was of the opinion that White Americans would give the negroes their rights only if they were aware of the facts. Although popular history supports Myrdal's notion like we saw in the desegregation rulings, Civil Rights Act (1964), and Voting Rights Act (1965), this isn't entirely true. Racist power started the civil-rights out of self-interest. Their interest declined once enough people of color were in spheres of power in America. Martin Luther King Jr. warned of this paradox of power but our generation has been ignoring his words.

Unlike what moral and educational suasion preach, racist policies must be changed before racist minds. Fighting for mental changes once policy changes have been made makes it possible for the antiracist power to succeed since it dissipates fear and allows the benefits to emerge. Real activism, therefore, produces policy and power change.

It is only policy changes that helps racial groups, not our donations to cultural and behavioral programs done primarily to make ourselves feel better. Just like the problems of racial injustice persist, we persistently do something superficial to satisfy ourselves. What if we had an outcome advocacy instead of a feelings advocacy to put real outcomes before our feelings of guilt?

I failed to persuade my BSU peers to act on the '106 campaign'. It was a campaign I had designed to free the 6 Black students at Jena High School facing unfair incarceration. I failed to convince my fellows because I failed to address their fears. Fear is a mirage, just like race is. It is merely the product of our imagination. However, *danger* is very real. To be an antiracist, we don't have to be fearless, rather we must be courageous. Unlike my peers who are fearful of what would happen if they resisted, I was fearful of what would happen if we didn't. I was fearful of the cowardice that the racist power has been inculcating into us for generations.

As I lay on my couch after the BSU officers voted down the 106 campaign, I was more convinced than ever in the power of education suasion. My enlightenment made me see my fellows as failure but was unable to help me recognize myself as the one failing them. The failure doctrine, failing to make change and then deflecting fault, was at play here. When people fail to consume our convoluted antiracist ideas, we blame their stupidity rather than our lack of clarity. Similarly, when our policy does not produce racial equity, we blame the people for not taking advantage of the new opportunity, not our flawed policy solution. The failure doctrine avoids self-blame and begets failure and racism. Whereas self-critique allows change from the constant insanity of doing the same thing and expecting different results.

Our antiracist power is anything but flexible and is too often bound by ideologies that are in turn bound by failed strategies of racial change. We care more about the moral and financial purity of our ideologies than about the results of policy changes that bring about equity for people in dire straits. Maybe things will change if our policies and strategies stemmed from problems instead of ideologies.

We use demonstrations and protests interchangeably, often to our own disadvantage. Unlike a demonstration, a protest organizes people for a prolonged campaign that ultimately brings a policy change. A demonstration, on the other hand, only publicizes a problem. Racist power typically ignores demonstrations unless it can't afford to do so such as during election season. Organizing and protesting is usually more difficult but more impactful than mobilizing and demonstrating. The most effective demonstrations, however, help people find the antiracist power within and provide the human and financial push to this newly awakened power to actually bring change.

In place of the 106 campaign, the BCU officers decided to organize a demonstration instead. These demonstrations, thought of as protests, had little effect to salvage the Jena 6. This was disheartening for some of my peers who expected to see a policy change as a result of these demonstrations. This failure to see the difference between demonstrations and protests then gives rise to the failure doctrine.

Chapter 17 - Success

Key Knowledge Pointers

- Success is a dark road that we fear but is nonetheless a place where antiracist power and policies dominate

- After realizing that my old concept of racism was faulty and that my previous vocabulary for racism was outdated, I made some necessary changes

- My second book *Stamped from the Beginning* unintentionally became an account of the history of racist policies in America as I witnessed the deaths, accusations, denials, and demonstrations for Black people all around me

At SUNY Oneonta, finance scholar Boyce Watkins lectured on *racism as a disease*. Feeling disturbed by this notion, I questioned him at the Q/A session. Caridad, with all her Puerto Rican feminism and antiracism, couldn't help but smile as I raised my hand. I became very close to Caridad after arriving as a dissertation fellow in 2008 and filling the Black history position left behind by her husband who died from cancer.

Success is a dark road that we fear but is nonetheless a place where antiracist power and policies dominate. Our willingness and courage to fight against the racist power is what will determine our stories. Caridad was a strong-willed antiracist and that helped strengthen my will as well. Like Kaila, Yaba and Weckea, Caridad ensured that I didn't return to my egotistic racist past, even after I had left Temple.

To Boyce Watkins, I asked, "Instead of describing racism as a disease, don't you think racism is more like an organ?" Sadly, my leading questions failed to lure Watkins into defending his idea of racism as a disease. That wasn't good because I wanted to engage him. I had closed myself off to any new ideas about racism that didn't feel good. It was hard to change my perspective without a fight unless it was done by someone like Kaila or Yaba whom I feared and respected. But how can antiracists then ask racists to change their minds when they themselves are so close-minded?

My concept of racism was derived from a book I read in graduate school. Authors Kwame Toure and political scientist Charles Hamilton described two forms of racism; individual whites overtly acting against individual Blacks, and covert acts by the White community against the Black community. They called the former *individual racism* (overt) and the latter *institutional racism* (covert). But by putting all Whites against all Blacks, this idea of racism ignored the fact that not all Whites benefited equally from racism. It also didn't take into account that some Black people exploited racism to gain wealth and power themselves. I myself thought of racism as an invisible immortal system instead of a living and mortal disease of cancer cells that could be killed with treatment.

This idea of a covert institutional racism is as eye-opening as it is misleading. It hides the specific policy choices that cause racial inequities and protects the policymakers as we collectively lash out at the system. Just like the culprits for individual racism can be identified specifically, the ones responsible for racist policies can also be singled out. In this way, all forms of racism are overt if we keep our antiracist eyes open to see the racist policies that cause racial inequities. The idea that institutional racism is often unseen and covert is the same as the post-racialist belief that racism hardly exists. Both keep our eyes closed as an antiracist.

I still occasionally use the words "institutional racism" and "systemic racism" and "structural racism" and "overt" and "covert" because they're a part of my old vocabulary for racism. But when we realize that old words no longer represent what we're trying to describe, we should turn to new words. When I now use 'racist policies' instead of 'institutional racism', I have in mind the average person who isn't exposed to knowledge about racism. I now believe that racism has always been terminal and curable, it has always been recognizable and mortal.

As I was looking for my first book to get published in two weeks' time, a teenager with a grey hooded sweatshirt bought watermelon juice and Skittles and was heading back to his home. The teenager took a shortcut through a particularly racist neighborhood which had 'seven' burglaries in 2011, when an armed watch-group organizer spotted him. Sensing that someone was following him, the teenager started running as the man zeroed-in on him while reporting to a 911 dispatcher. Combating each other as the teenager tried to protect himself and the man fought to 'apprehend' the 'criminal', the trigger was squeezed and ended the teenager's life. The man's claim for self-defense was later granted by a jury in 2013.

I didn't plan for my second book to be a history of racist ideas. But the deaths, accusations, denials, and demonstrations for others like that teenager Trayvon Martin gave me the courage to research for my second book *Stamped from the Beginning*. I gathered every racist idea that I could from history and, in doing so, realized that I myself had been doing a lot of this unintentionally. Thus, my mission to unearth America's life of racist ideas turned into a lifelong mission to be an antiracist.

Although I had cleansed my mind, I didn't cleanse my body. But then I couldn't worry about my own Black body when other Black bodies around me were butchered by police officers and when the racists blamed the dead ones as their families cried and numbed at their loss.

Chapter 18 - Survival

Key Knowledge Pointers

- My wife's Sadiqa's struggle with cancer overturned my previous thinking about ignorance as the source of racist ideas, racist ideas as the source of racist policies and mental change as the principal solution to the problem of racism

- My second book *Stamped from the Beginning*, therefore, addressed focusing on policy change instead of mental change

- As I was diagnosed with stage 4 metastatic colon cancer, I realized that Our world is also suffering from metastatic cancer of racism

- Just like I fought with my colon cancer, we can also fight the cancer of racism by treating it the same way we would any other cancer

Sadiqa's struggle with invasive breast cancer and my own study of racism consumed my life over the final months of 2013 and a good part of 2014 and 2015. We were married to each other by then but everything came crashing down afterwards. A serious complication occurred as we tried to freeze embryos before the cancer treatment began. Sadiqa had to go through multiple chemotherapy sessions and three surgeries before she finally won. However, months after Sadiqa survived stage-2 breast cancer, Ma was diagnosed with stage-1 breast cancer. During those years, I was torn between taking care of Sadiqa and helping with my mother. Any free time was spent drowning in the stack of racist ideas that I had collected.

I had trouble recognizing it at first but Sadiqa's courage inspired me to acknowledge the source of these racist ideas as not ignorance and hate, but self-interest. This discovery overturned my previous thinking about ignorance as the source of racist ideas, racist ideas as the source of racist policies and mental change as the principal solution to the problem of racism. Historically, racist policymakers developed racist policies out of self-interest and then produced racist ideas to defend these policies. As the common man consumed these racist ideas, hate and ignorance was born. Thus treating ignorance and hate and expecting racism to suddenly shrink seemed like treating a cancer patient's symptoms and expecting the tumors to shrink. As long as the underlying cause of self-interest remains, curing ignorance and hate would do no good. In this context, I recognized that educational and moral suasion is not only a bad strategy, it's suicidal.

My second book *Stamped from the Beginning*, therefore, addressed focusing on policy change instead of mental change. As I took this message out on the street, I was being called out for my own hypocrisy. People asked "What are you doing to change policy?" Finding the answer to this question led me to abandon the suasionist inside me. Instead of researching and educating to change minds, I started doing the same to change policy. The insights I gathered influenced me to build residential fellowship programs by combining a team of scholars and policy experts with the nation's most politically-aware student body. The teams would work on identifying racist policies, innovating antiracist policies to replace them and then broadcasting, testing and instituting these policies both nationally and internationally.

After I've briefed my peers at American University about my vision, a White middle-aged man posted Confederate flags inside several buildings and outside my classroom. I ignored him as well as my unexplained weight loss. But my condition worsened as I started throwing up during Thanksgiving followed by bloody diarrhea that won't stop. Both Sadiqa and I didn't think it was anything serious as we went to get myself checked out. But the precautionary colonoscopy revealed that I had cancer. I was comforted by my family upon hearing the news and thought of my wife's, dad's and Ma's fights with cancer. They survived, and I can too. The next day, I was informed that I had stage 4 metastatic cancer. Maybe my enthusiasm to fight this disease was in vain after all.

Our world is also suffering from metastatic cancer but many of us deny their nation's racial inequities and their racist policies. They flatly renounce the cancer of racism as it spreads and threatens their own lives as well as those of their loved ones. Denial, like the popular strategy of suasion, is equally suicidal.

Shortly after my diagnosis, I wrote an article arguing that the heartbeat of racism is denial. However, personally I was still in denial of the severity of my cancer. The denial of my ability to fight with cancer wasn't much different from the denial of those that doubted our ability to fight against racism. So I prepared myself for the fight and battled with cancer as my two-year old Black girl grew into a phenomenal woman, as I wrote for *The Atlantic* like W.E.B. Du Bois and as I finished and shared this book with the world.

In late January 2018, my chemo injections started. Although I could barely do anything with the chemo, I pushed myself out of bed and exercised my mind and body. I knew that pain is usually essential to healing and when it comes to healing America of racism there is no progress without pain as well. By the end of the summer of 2018, my doctors took out the shrunken tumors and were shocked by my recovery. My chances to land in the 12% of people who survived stage-4 colon cancer were strong.

We can also survive metastatic cancer. What if we treated racism the same way as cancer? What has historically proven effective against racism is the same to what has been effective at fighting cancer. What if we connected the treatment plans of cancer with racism? Treat the body of racism with chemotherapy of antiracist policies that shrink the tumors of racial inequities and kill the cancer cells of racism. Then remove any remaining racist policies like doctors remove shrunken tumors. Ensure there are no cancer cells remaining and that the body consumes healthy foods for thought and regular exercising of antiracist ideas to prevent recurrence. Monitor the body closely when it is known that racial inequity previously existed and detect and treat a recurrence early.

But we must first believe that we and our societies can be antiracists from this day onwards. Racist ideas aren't natural to the human mind neither are racist inequities inevitable. Racism is a cancer we've caught that isn't as much as 600 years old yet it is one of the fastest-spreading cancers in humanity. However, if we fight to create an antiracist world against all odds, then we give humanity a chance to survive and be free one day.

The End.